THE FIRST BOOK OF TENOR SOLOS PART III

compiled by Joan Frey Boytim

G. SCHIRMER, Inc.

DISTRIBUTED BY

HAL•LEONARD®
CORPORATION

7777 W. BLUEMOUND RD. P.O. BOX 13819 MILWAUKEE, WI 53213

PREFACE

The First Book of Solos series has been compiled to meet requests of voice teachers who have expressed a need for more beginning vocal literature similar to the "Part I" and "Part II" books. This repertoire speaks to students who may have successfully sung songs from the *Easy Songs for Beginning Singers* series. Those students who have used *The First Book of Solos — Part I and Part II*, may still find that this level of song material is appropriate before venturing into the volumes of *The Second Book of Solos*. This new "Part III" may also suffice as a beginning book for certain students, or serve as a companion to "Part I" and "Part II." Since the level is the same for *The First Book of Solos — Part I, Part II and Part III*, a student can begin in any of the books.

The first two volumes were released in 1991 and 1993. Since then, some excellent songs have passed into the "Public Domain" category. It is significant that songs such as "The Green Cathedral," "Waters Ripple and Flow," "A Brown Bird Singing," "When I Think Upon the Maidens," "The Ships of Arcady," "May-Day Carol," and "The Time for Making Songs Has Come" have become available for young singers.

The anthologies in "Part III" contain 34 to 36 songs appropriate to specific voice types, and in suitable keys. The basic format provides songs of many styles from the baroque era into the 20th century. In addition to many familiar standard art songs, there are a number of unfamiliar gems, such as "The Bubble Song," the trilogy "At the Zoo," "Bluebird," "The Little Old Lady in Lavender Silk," "Maidens Are Like the Wind," "Sing a Song of Sixpence," and "When Big Profundo Sang Low C." In keeping with the original format, there are many American and British songs, as well as a good sampling of Italian, German and French art songs (with singable translations). Some favorites include "Invictus," "Come Back to Sorrento," "Vilia," and "I Walked Today Where Jesus Walked." As in the other books of the series, a few sacred solos are included. Many songs in "Part III" were previously obtainable in only sheet form or have been long out of print. In order to include songs represented by the 1916 to 1922 year span, several of the accompaniments and songs may prove to be a bit more of a challenge than in "Part I" and "Part II."

The First Book of Solos — Part III concludes this series of five books for each voice type, with no song duplication (*The First Book of Solos — Part I, Part II, Part III, The Second Book of Solos — Part I, Part II*). The number of songs in the twenty volumes totals 668. The average number of songs presented for each voice numbers approximately 167. This presents a wide smorgasbord of vocal literature for studio and performance use for student singers at most any age.

G. Schirmer is to be commended for allowing this series of vocal solos to grow substantially. Wherever I meet teachers who have used these many books, they express profound thanks for them, and acknowledge that their availability makes repertoire demands so much easier to manage. May you and your students enjoy the new choices made available in this anthology.

Joan Frey Boytim
June, 2005

CONTENTS

4 ARISE, O LORD   Leon Abbott Hoffmeister

8 AUF FLÜGELN DES GESANGES (On Wings of Song)   Felix Mendelssohn

12 BEHOLD, WHAT MANNER OF LOVE   Don Humphreys

18 BON JOUR, MA BELLE!   Arthur Henry Behrend

24 THE CHILDREN   Theodore Chanler

27 COME, FAIR ROSINA   Francis Hopkinson

30 DOUCE DAME JOLIE (Sweet-heart, gentle and pretty)   Guillaume de Machaut

32 DOWN BY THE RIVERSIDE   Old English Folksong, arranged by Richard Manning

36 I HEAR YOU CALLING ME   Charles Marshall

40 J'AI TANT DE CHOSES À VOUS DIRE (I've a Host of Things to Tell You)
Giacomo Gotifredo Ferrari

44 KITTY, MY LOVE, WILL YOU MARRY ME?   Old Ulster Song, arranged by Herbert Hughes

48 DER KUß (The Kiss)   Ludwig van Beethoven

60 THE LARK IN CLEAR AIR   Irish Air, arranged by William Arms Fisher

52 DER LEIERMANN (The Organ Grinder)   Franz Schubert

56 LET THE HEAVENS REJOICE   Frank La Forge

66 MÄDCHEN SIND WIE DER WIND (Maidens are like the wind)
Johann Karl Gottfried Loewe

63 NOW SLEEPS THE CRIMSON PETAL   Roger Quilter

70 'O SOLE MIO! (My Sunshine)   Eduardo di Capua

72 PEACE I LEAVE WITH YOU   J. Varley Roberts

78 SAILOR'S SONG   Franz Joseph Haydn

84 A SEASONAL THANKSGIVING   Eric H. Thiman

88 SEEK YE THE LORD   J. Varley Roberts

96 SELVE AMICHE, OMBROSE PIANTE (Friendly forest, ye shadowy arches)   Antonio Caldara

100 SHADY GROVE   American Folksong, arranged by Celius Dougherty

105 SHOES   Kathleen Lockhart Manning

108 SING A SONG OF SIXPENCE   Herbert Hughes

116 THE SLEIGH   Richard Kountz

113 SONNET D'AMOUR (A Love Sonnet)   Francis Thomé

120 STÄNDCHEN (Serenade)   Robert Franz

134 TORNA A SURRIENTO (Come Back to Sorrento)   Ernesto de Curtis

124 TRADE WINDS   Frederick Keel

128 WEHMUT (Sadness)   Robert Schumann

130 WHEN I THINK UPON THE MAIDENS   Michael Head

ARISE, O LORD

Adapted from Psalm 9

Leon Abbott Hoffmeister

AUF FLÜGELN DES GESANGES
(On Wings of Song)

Heinrich Heine
English version by Alice Mattullath

Felix Mendelssohn
(1809-1847)

BEHOLD, WHAT MANNER OF LOVE

I John 3:1-3

Don Humphreys

we should be called the sons of God, be - hold, what man - ner of

love, _____ be-hold, what man - ner of love _____ the

Fa - ther hath bestowed up-on us, that we should be called the sons of God:

there-fore the world knoweth us not, _____ for it knew, it knew Him not.

Lento

mp

Be - lov - ed, now are we the sons of God,

now are we the sons of God, ___ and it doth not yet ap-

pear what we shall be, what we shall be: ___ but we

know that, when He shall ap-pear, but we know that, when He

shall ap-pear, we shall be _____ like Him, _____ we shall

be _____ like Him.

And he who hath this hope in Him, and he who hath this

hope in Him pu - ri - fi - eth him - self,

e - ven as He is pure,

BON JOUR, MA BELLE!

Guy Eden

Arthur Henry Behrend
(1853-1935)

There were

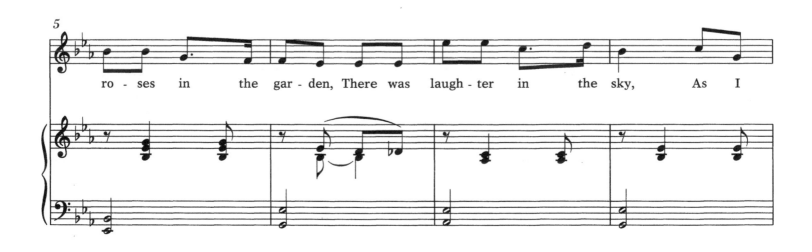

ro - ses in the gar - den, There was laugh - ter in the sky, As I

met that lit - tle maid - en, And she shy - ly passed me by, And my

heart went pit - a - pat - ter On that gold - en sum - mer day, As the

rall. *ten.* *a tempo*

sun - light played a - round her In her dain - ty robe of grey. She was

French, and I was Eng - lish, So what was a man to do? But I

f rall. *rit.*

strug - gled to re - mem - ber All the lit - tle French I knew?_____ "Bon

Then I watched her as the blush - es Dyed her cheeks with ro - sy red, As with

down - cast eyes she lis - tened To the words that I had said, And my

heart went pit - a - pat - ter As she raised those eyes di - vine, And I

THE CHILDREN

Leonard Feeney

Theodore Chanler
(1902-1961)

Words used by exclusive permission.

—— And when we grow old-er, what do you sup-pose____ Will be-come of the chil-dren?

sempre f

Will there be chil-dren a-gain, When we who are chil-dren are wo-men and

men? Yes! Sure-ly the world will love

poco a poco dim.

chil-dren no less; Chil-dren will come when we chil-dren are gone,____

COME, FAIR ROSINA

Francis Hopkinson
(1737-1791)

Andante ♩ = 88

mf

poco rit.

a tempo

mf

1. Come, fair Ros - i - na, come _____ a - way, _ Long since stern Win - ter's storms _ have _ ceased, _ See Na - ture in _____ her best _____ ar - ray _ In - vites us _ to _____ her
2. At noon we'll seek the wild - wood's shade, _ And o'er the path - less ver - dure _ rove, _ Or near _____ a mos - sy foun - tain laid, _ At - tend the _ mus - ic

DOUCE DAME JOLIE
(Sweet-heart, gentle and pretty)

Guillaume de Machaut
(c.1300-1377)

to Lester Hodges

DOWN BY THE RIVERSIDE

Old English Folk-Song

Arranged by
Richard Manning

ment - ing, sigh - ing, cry - ing, for her own true

love. "What

Molto meno mosso, quasi adagio

makes you sigh __ and __ cry, my fair pret - ty maid?" __ said

I, "I am la - ment - ing __ for my own true

allargando   *con sentimento*   *a tempo*

love, I am la - ment - ing, sigh - ing, cry - ing, for my

own true love." ___

I HEAR YOU CALLING ME

Harold Harford

Charles Marshall
(1857-1927)

J'AI TANT DE CHOSES À VOUS DIRE
(I've a Host of Things to Tell You)

Lamquet
English version by George Cooper

Giacomo Gotifredo Ferrari
(1759-1842)

28
Car ce ma-tin j'ai ren-con-tré Les deux pre-miè-res hi-ron -
For, on this morn-ing, I have met Two ear-ly swal-lows, wing-ing

31
del - les Ré-pa-rant leur nid ____ dé-la-bré.
light - ly, To re-pair their nest, ____ emp-ty yet!

34
L'air est pur, il fait bon de vi - vre, A - vril, ain-si qu'un vin nou -
Pure the air, and so sweet with glad - ness! A - pril! it thrills like wind, so

37
veau, Trou-ble mes re-gards et m'en i - vre, J'ai des
new! Long-ing thoughts a-wak - en my sad - ness, Dreams are

KITTY, MY LOVE, WILL YOU MARRY ME?

Old Ulster Song

Arranged by Herbert Hughes
(1882-1937)

Allegro. *(In lilting fashion.)*

Kit-ty, my love, will you mar-ry me? Kit-ty, my love, will you go, O!

Kit-ty, my love, will you mar-ry me? Ei-ther say Yes or say No, O!

DER KUß
(The Kiss)

Christian Felix Weisse

Ludwig van Beethoven
(1770–1827)

Allegretto *mit Lebhaftigkeit, jedoch nicht in geschwindem Zeitmaasse, und scherzend vorgetragen*

Ich war bei Chlo - en ganz al - lein, und _
I was a - lone with my _ love, And I

küs - sen _ wollt' ich sie, und küs - sen, küs - sen,
wan - ted _ to _ kiss and hug her, hold her,

DER LEIERMANN
(The Organ Grinder)
from *Winterreise*

Wilhelm Müller

Franz Schubert
(1797-1828)

steht ihm nim - mer still.
turns and turns a - way.

Wun - der-li - cher Al - ter, soll ich mit dir __
Won - der-ful old min-strel shall I go with __

gehn?
you?

Willst zu mei - nen Lie - dern dei - ne Lei - er dreh'n? __
Will you to my dit - ties play the mu - sic too? ___

to Ralph Quist

LET THE HEAVENS REJOICE

Adapted from Psalm 96

Frank La Forge
(1879-1953)

Let the heav-ens re-joice!

Sing, sing un-to the Lord, all the earth!

Sing un-to the Lord, bless His name;

show forth His sal - va - tion from day to day.

Hon - or and maj - es - ty are be -

fore Him. Strength and beau - ty are in His sanc - tu - a - ry.

THE LARK IN CLEAR AIR

Samuel Ferguson

Irish Air "Kathleen Nowlan"
Arranged by William Arms Fisher
(1861-1948)

to Mrs. E.P. Balmain

NOW SLEEPS THE CRIMSON PETAL

Alfred Tennyson

Roger Quilter
(1877–1953)

Moderato quasi andantino ♩ = 60 tempo rubato

Now sleeps the crim-son pe-tal, not the white; ____

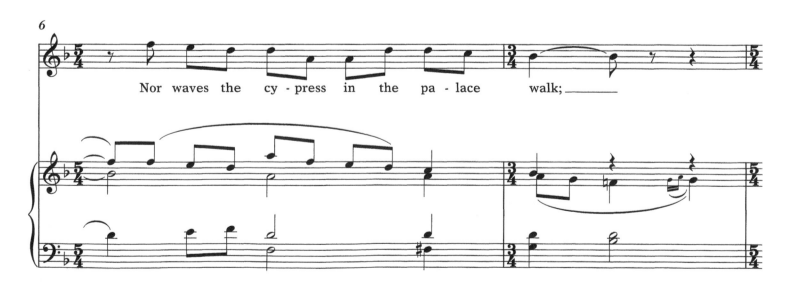

Nor waves the cy-press in the pa-lace walk; ____

MÄDCHEN SIND WIE DER WIND
(Maidens are like the wind)

Johann Karl Gottfried Loewe
(1796-1869)

Quickly *(Geschwind)*

Maid - ens are like the wind,
Mäd - chen sind wie der Wind,

Their re - gard be - stow - ing
schen - ken oft im Scher - ze

Now on me, then on thee,
heu - te mir, mor - gen dir,

Like a leaf - let blow - ing.
flat - ter - haft ihr Her - ze.

O be-ware! have a care: When she seems be - guil-ing!
Trau-e__nicht! *die - se spricht:* *„Lieb - chen, dir zu die - nen!"*

Trick - y lies, mock-ing eyes Lurk be-hind her smil - ing.
Schmei-che - lei, Heu-che - lei lacht aus ih - ren Mie - nen.

Ne'er sup-pose, when she goes
Wo__ sie gehn, wo sie stehn,

That her kiss is bind-ing;
wenn sie dich auch küs-sen,

If she choose to a - buse,
wer - den sie dort und hie

Fault she can be find-ing.
was zu ta-deln wis-sen.

Tho' the bliss
Schön und rund

of her kiss,
lockt ihr Mund,

Leads to joy - ous sigh-ing,
zwar mit sü - ssem Schal-le,

Hid-den there, nev-er fear,
schlau ver - deckt a - ber steckt

Bit-ter gall is ly - ing.
doch im Her - zen Gal - le.

'O SOLE MIO!
(My Sunshine)

Giovanni Capurro
English version by Henry G. Chapman

Eduardo di Capua
(1864-1917)

PEACE I LEAVE WITH YOU

John 14:27; 16:6, 33

J. Varley Roberts

SAILOR'S SONG

Anne Hunter

Franz Joseph Haydn
(1732-1809)

fear - less of the __ rush - ing blast he care - less whist - les to __ the __ gale.

Rat - tling ropes and

roll - ing __ seas!   Hur - ly

bur - ly, hur - ly bur - ly!   War nor

death

can him dis - please, can him dis - please.

Hur - ly bur - ly! Hur - ly

bur - ly, hur - ly bur - ly, hur - ly bur - ly! War nor

death

can him dis - please, can him dis - please, can him dis -

A SEASONAL THANKSGIVING

E. Byne Haggerty*

Eric H. Thiman
(1900-1975)

* Words printed by special permission.

For mel - low tints of au - tumn days: For fruits which line _____ the bri - dle ways: For hills which shim - mer in the haze, Our heart-felt thanks, _____ O Lord.

SEEK YE THE LORD

Isaiah 55:6,7

J. Varley Roberts

Seek ye the Lord while He may___ be found,

call ye up - on Him while He ___ is near;

seek ye the Lord while He may ___ be found,

cresc. molto

call ye up - on Him while He is near:

mf

Let the

pp

wick - ed for-sake his way,____ and the un - right - eous man his

p espressivo

thoughts,_ and re - turn un-to the Lord, re -

rall.

turn un-to the Lord,

a tempo

may __ be found, __ call ye up - on Him while

He is near, seek ye the Lord while He

may __ be __ found, call ye up - on Him while He

mer - cy, and a - bun - dant - ly par - don,

He will have

mer - cy, and a - bun - dant-ly par - don. A - men.

SELVE AMICHE, OMBROSE PIANTE

(Friendly forest, ye shadowy arches)

English version by Joan Boytim

Antonio Caldara
(1670-1736)

SHADY GROVE

American Folksong
Arranged by
Celius Dougherty
(1902-1986)

Allegro molto ♩ = 120

Sha - dy grove, my true love,

Sha - dy grove I know, Sha - dy grove, my__ true__ love, I'm

Sha - dy grove, my true love I'm bound for the sha - dy grove.

Wish I had a fid - dle string, made of gold - en twine, Ev - 'ry tune I'd pick on it is "I wish that girl were mine." Sha - dy grove, my true love,

p cantando

with pedal

mf

no pedal

Sha - dy grove I know, Sha - dy grove, my _ true _ love, I'm

bound for the sha - dy grove. _____

Peach - es in the sum - mer - time, Ap - ples in the fall, If I

molto marcato
p

can't have the girl _ I _ love I won't have none at all.

Sha - dy grove, my true love, Sha - dy grove I know,

mf

with pedal

Sha - dy grove, my __ true __ love, I'm bound for the sha - dy

grove. _____

no pedal

to Alice Forsythe Mosher

SHOES

Kathleen Lockhart Manning
(1890-1951)

SING A SONG OF SIXPENCE

Herbert Hughes
(1882-1937)

Allegro vivace ♩ = 144

p delicatamente

Sing a song of six-pence, A pock-et full of rye,

Four-and-twen-ty black birds baked in a pie. When the pie was op - ened the

birds be-gan to sing, Was-n't that a dain-ty dish to set be-fore a King!

58
baked _ in a pie. When the pie was op - ened the birds be - gan to sing _____

61
Was-n't that a dain - ty _ dish to   When the pie was op - ened the

8va -

64
birds be - gan to   Was-n't that a dain - ty _ dish to   set be - fore _ a King.

8 -

67
(spoken)
Was-n't that a dain-ty dish?

r.h.

SONNET D'AMOUR
(A Love Sonnet)

A. de Saineville

Francis Thomé
(1850-1909)

Largamente

dolce

Sous le so - leil,__ qui les __ i - ri - se,
Soft in the sun __ thy gold - en tress - es,

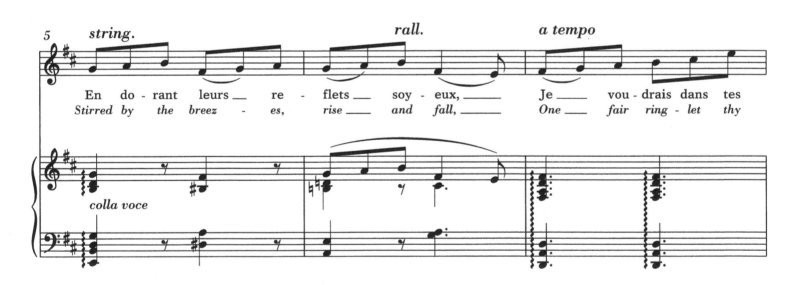

string. *rall.* *a tempo*

En do - rant leurs __ re - flets __ soy - eux, __ Je __ vou - drais dans tes
Stirred by the breez - es, rise __ and fall, __ One __ fair ring - let thy

colla voce

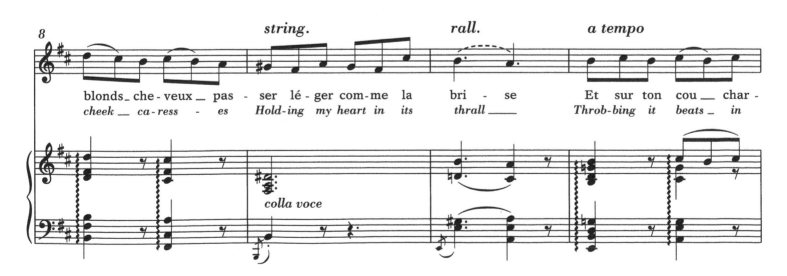

string. *rall.* *a tempo*

blonds_che - veux_ pas - ser lé - ger com - me la bri - se Et sur ton cou __ char -
cheek __ ca - ress - es Hold - ing my heart in its thrall __ Throb-bing it beats __ in

colla voce

to Irma Carpenter

THE SLEIGH
À la Russe

Ivor Tchervanow

Richard Kountz
(1896-1950)

snow so cold and crisp and light, With sharp winds blow-ing, We are go-ing

On-ward through the night, Hey - - a -

o - - la! Hey - - a - - o - - la!

Light - ly fly - ing o'er the snow, With a hey hah, hah, hah, ho, hah, ho! With

sleigh - bells ring - ing, Gai - ly sing - ing, Mer - ri - ly we go.

Ho, hal - lo! Mer - ri - ly on we go.

STÄNDCHEN
(Serenade)

Friedrich Rückert

Robert Franz
(1815-1892)

TRADE WINDS

John Masefield

Frederick Keel
(1871-1954)

With a smooth flowing rhythm

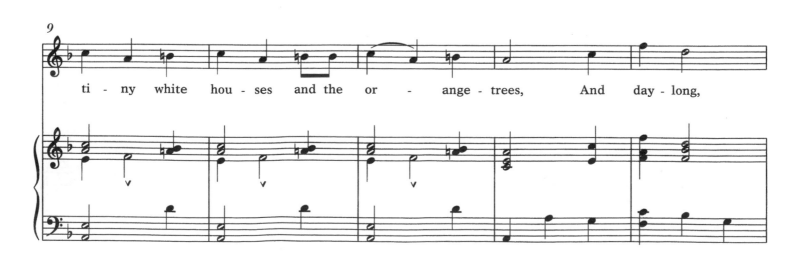

tune   Of the qui - et voice call - ing me,   The

long   low croon___ Of the stea - dy Trade__ Winds blow -

- - - - - - - - - - ing.___

WEHMUT
(Sadness)

Joseph von Eichendorff
English version by Joan Boytim

Robert Schumann
(1810-1856)

Früh - lings-luft, der Sehn - sucht Lied er-schal - len aus ih - res Ker - kers
night ___ air, a long - ing song that breaks ___ the chains ___ of love's des -

Gruft.
pair. *We all can sense the glad - ness when ev - 'ry thing ___ is*

freut, doch kei - ner fühlt die Schmer - zen, im Lied das tie - fe
joy. *Yet no one feels the sad - ness the song can-not de -*

Leid.
stroy.

WHEN I THINK UPON THE MAIDENS

Philip Ashbrooke

Michael Head
(1900-1976)

Debts my heart can ne - ver pay.

Do they scorn me now I won - der, Did they take it as a game?

Flor - a, O - live, And the oth - ers, How I ha - ted all their broth-ers!

TORNA A SURRIENTO
(Come Back to Sorrento)

Gian Battista de Curtis

Ernesto de Curtis
(1875-1937)

che me, de -sto, fa so - gnar. _____ Sen - ti co -me lie -ve sa - le
Till I'm dream-ing though a - wake. _____ See the love -ly dew -y gar - den,
non lo sa di -men -ti - car. _____ Ve -di co -me le Si - re - ne
But may nev -er find the like. _____ See the Si - rens all a - round you,

dai giar -di - ni o -dor d'a -ran - ci: un pro -fu -mo non v'ha e - gua - le
Breath-ing scent of or -ange -blos -soms; Such a sweet and gra -cious per - fume
or ti guar -da -no in -can -ta - te, par che vo -glia -no a te so - la
Look-ing on you so en -chant - ed; And so dear -ly do they love you

per chi pal -pi -ta d'a -mor! _____ E tu di -ci "Io par -to, ad -di - o!"
That it en -ters in one's heart. _____ And you say "Good-bye, I'm go - ing,"
dol -ci co -se mor -mo - rar _____
That they now would kiss your lips. _____